Meanwhile, in Other News....

A Graphic Look at Politics in the Empire of Money, Sex & Scandal

Matt Wuerker

Common Courage Press   *Monroe, ME*

Cataloging in publication data is available from the publisher.

Common Courage Press
Box 702
Monroe, ME 04951

207-525-0900 fax: 207-525-3068
orders-info@commoncouragepress.com
http://www.commoncouragepress.com

First Printing

FOR SARAH

MY LOVE, MY MUSE, MY SPELLCHECK.

Foreword

Politics are funny. Politics are serious. The news is a joke. The news is not a joke. All these statements are true.

I believe any good satire reflects all the above simultaneously. Satire is cynical and often profane, and at the same time it's idealistic and heartfelt. It comes from hoping for the best and being outraged at how far short we fall of it. Finding the humor in our ineptitudes, but not losing sight of the fact that things are also serious — that's the trick.

It's funny that Rush Limbaugh is always claiming to be "in the relentless pursuit of the truth." It's not funny that every day he fills the heads of millions of listeners with misogynist dreck, corporatist propaganda and other reactionary bull-hockey that panders to the worst reflexes of our national pysche.

It's funny when Newt Gingrich fancies himself the great anthropologist and explains that feminism is doomed because women aren't the giraffe-hunting types and that women need to stay out of "the trenches" or risk "infections." It's not funny when Newt wins the leadership of the Congress and sets to work making good on his Contract with Corporate America — selling legislation to the highest coporate bidders.

It's funny when the media paint Bill Clinton as some wild-eyed liberal when realistically you'd have to put him somewhere to the right of Richard Nixon. It's not funny when Clinton works hard to pass NAFTA and GATT, further lining the pockets of Wall Street investors at the expense of the U.S. factory workers. It's even less funny when he "reforms" welfare and throws millions of families into poverty.

Sometimes it's hard to keep a sense of humor about it all, but then all you have to do is remember that humorists have God on their side. I've become absolutely certain that God is neither Muslim, Christian, Jewish or Buddist — she has to be a Satirist. How else can you explain The Clinton-Starr-Lewinsky Law and Libido Circus? Dan Quayle For President? Reality has reached such absurd heights of farce that it outstrips the satirist's ablility to satirize. God is clearly messing with us. It's something out of Homer, in which some god is up there mischievously testing how far we can be pushed before we lose our minds completely and just run the ship up onto the rocks.

Not getting distracted is important here. All the stained dress jokes may be hilarious but are completely beside the point. As Molly Ivins has noted, it's a shell game. The trick is keeping your eye on the pea — the elevated romantic temperatures in the Oval Office, as entertaining as they are, will pass; the elevated global warming may not. There are big things shaking down and it's important to pay attention.

These cartoons are my effort to stay with that pea. I hope they deal with the serious issues — and I hope they're funny.

Matt Wuerker, September 1998

Contents

Don't Forget Mr. Humor

In my opinion, the last, great journalists in America are those dedicated few whose work is in the noble tradition of our country's revolutionary pamphleteers: ink-stained champions of the cartoonist's craft. And none is better at this craft than the man whose work you hold in your hands: Matt Wuerker.

Freethinking, freewheeling souls like Matt not only grasp the core truth in the issue of the day, but they draw us a picture of it! Better yet, they reach us not merely through the mind, the heart, the gut—but especially through the funny bone.

Progressives too often overlook this crucial body part when trying to convey our ideas, ideals, facts and viewpoint to the larger public. I urge you to peruse *Meanwhile, in Other News...* not only for the substance and perspective he brings to so many timely issues, but also for the way he delivers the message. Matt teaches us that Mr. Humor is not our enemy. Indeed, he is our friend. So be not afraid of Mr. Humor. He is there to keep us sane and also to open doors for us. When he arrives in your head do not reject Mr. Humor.

Yes, working for social change is serious business, and yes, indeed, it is a grim world out there, but hey, nobody likes a grouch.

Whether your humor is broad, boisterous, and bodacious—or dry, sly, wry, and petite, whatever you've got, turn that little sucker loose, please. I commend to you my own personal credo, which is: "You can fight the gods and still have fun." After all, we are engaged in the glorious work of battling the Powers That Be on behalf of the Powers That Oughta Be, and we need to enjoy that. So turn your joy loose!

Another tip: the very first rule of communication is know what it is you want to say. What is your message? And by message I don't mean that full truckload of information and issues that you want to dump out on the American people, but what it all boils down to. So folks can get it, get it in their hearts, get it in their guts, because that is after all what truly motivates each and every one of us. Well, for me our progressive message boils down to a small set of big values, indeed the founding values of our people and our nation—very, very radical values: economic fairness, social justice, equal opportunity for all people, and good stewardship of this globe. There are hundreds of different issues that fit within this framework of values, values that the American people already hold deeply within themselves and that cannot be shaken even by the money and the media conglomerates in our society.

Let's take one issue as an example of this: economic disparity. Because there is so much disparity in our land today, a lot of progressives want to talk about redistribution of wealth. My advice? Please don't. A phrase like "redistribution of wealth" is policy wonkishness at its worst. It sounds like sex talk for economists. Using this issue of economic disparity, let me give you a six step recovery program to heal the heartbreak of wonkishness.

Step number one: We're not really talking about redistribution of wealth, we're talking about economic fairness, the broadly-held *value* of fairness. In this case, it can be expressed something like this: the workaday majority of American folks are working harder and longer than ever before, producing greater wealth than ever before, yet getting less and less in return. That is not fair, pure and simple. That reality resonates in the hearts of every American in the United States.

Okay, you've established the values, so now you can take a small step toward wonkishness. You can resort to numbers, to document this unfairness. Not too many numbers, just a couple. Something like this: Wall Street and Washington alike agree, indeed even boast, that the '90s are a time of unprecedented growth and prosperity, yet 80% of us have lost income. Eight out of ten. It's not just the rich versus the poor anymore, it's the rich versus the rest of us. The middle class, indeed the opportunity to be middle class, is being knocked down. The money that's being generated by all of us is being hauled off by the privileged few. And then, to take one more little wonkish step, you can note that in the past decade we, the American people, have generated $12 trillion in new wealth. What have we gotten out of that? What is our percentage of that, the percentage of new wealth going to the majority, eight out of ten of us? We got 1% of it.

That divides out to less than keeping up with inflation, which is why we're falling behind. The 99% went to the privileged ones at the top.

Step number three (here's Mr. Humor knocking): Now is the time to rivet this unfairness with a memorable punctuation point. I'm partial to the zinger, to the one-liner. Something like, "Sure, Wall Street's whizzing. It's whizzing on you and me." People get that. Or maybe a pop culture reference. Instead of some long quotation from Goethe or Nieztsche, why not Ray Charles? He's good. He had a song that wailed, "Them that's got is them that gets, and I ain't got nothing yet." Again, the American people know that in their own experience. You do not have to explain it to them.

Step number four: now is the time to personalize the unfairness, to put a face to it. How many of you made $282,000 last year? Less than 1% of the American people make that much money, but one who did is Mikey Eisner, the head Mousketeer of Disney, Inc. He made $282,000—not for the year, not for a month. He didn't make $282,000 a week, or even for a day, he made $282,000 *an hour*. Plus a car. Meanwhile he was knocking down the health care benefits to the minimum wage workers who work at Disneyland and Disney World.

Step number five (it's time for Mr. Humor again): Another zinger. Something like, "Some of these executives like Michael Eisner are getting so rich they can afford to air condition Hell. And the way they're acting, they'd better be setting some money aside for that project."

Final step, number six: put a tag on the unfairness. Something like this, "Economists have a technical term to characterize this transference of wealth from the bottom to the top. The technical term is 'stealing.' " Faster than a hog eats supper, they're stealing from us. But the real term for what's happening is class war. See, now we put our term to it. It's class war. The privileged few are waging an unrelenting, take-no-prisoners class war against the middle class and the poor people in this country, and it's time we begin to fight back against it.

Having gone through this six step program, you can now afford to be wonkish, because you have folks' attention. You've set the stage for the solutions that you want to discuss, from living-wage campaigns to third party politics, from taxing the stock transactions of the elites to fighting for re-chartering of American corporations. Then you can get into the details of it.

Using Mr. Humor, as Matt Wuerker shows in the following pages, allows us to reach not only the beansprout eaters, but also the snuff dippers in our society. It allows them to hear our agenda without knee-jerk prejudice. After all, the progressive agenda is really a mainstream All-American agenda. What you want is exactly what most Americans want. We want our country back, back from the greed heads and the dead heads, from the speculators and the spoilers, from the bosses and the bankers, from the big shots and the bas-

tards who are running over us. Say that to the people. Say it plainly, as widely and as loudly as you possibly can. Get the biggest microphone that you can possible grab, and say it again and again . . . and then smile. Smile! Not only will the workaday folks in this country understand and appreciate your smile and what you're saying, but that smile will also drive the powers that be absolutely crazy. Of course, that's a pretty short ride for most of 'em.

Jim Hightower, September 1998

CHAPTER 1

FALSE HOPES

The End of Liberalism as We Know It.

START FLIP BOOK HERE

1

4

6

Mighty Bill at Bat

M. WUERKER

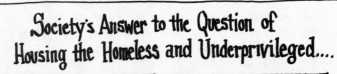

Society's Answer to the Question of
Housing the Homeless and Underprivileged....

1970   2000

12

THE UPDATED
POLITICAL TAXONOMY

TRIANGULATED
CLINTOMELEON
(neodemocraticus finger-to-the-windus)

GREAT WESTERN
DOLEFUL-O
(dour downbeatus doldrumus)

PRICKLY TONGUED
PEROTCUPINE
(billionarius-of-the-peoplius)

15

17

18

19

20

CHAPTER 2

THE BEST DEMOCRACY MONEY CAN BUY

WE'VE SIMPLIFIED THE REPUBLICAN CONTRACT TO ITS ONE CENTRAL CORE POINT...

ENOUGH OF **ONE MAN ONE VOTE**

CHAIRMAN OF THE BOARD

IT'S TIME FOR **ONE DOLLAR ONE VOTE!**

M. WUERKER

IT'S TIME WE DECLARED AMERICA A...

MONACRACY

NO MORE SILLY PRETENSE ABOUT THE GOVERNMENT REPRESENTING THE PEOPLE! IN OUR NEW MONACRACY GOVERNMENT WILL SIMPLY AND DIRECTLY REPRESENT —

MONEY!

COME ON SENATOR, MUST I LEAD YOU EVERYWHERE?! GIDDY-UP!!

RESTRUCTURE GOVERNMENT! NO MORE PESKY MIDDLEMEN — NO MORE NEEDING TO BUY EXPENSIVE POLITICIANS OR PUBLIC OPINION IN A SYSTEM THAT MERELY FAVORS THE WEALTHY.

HERE SIR, YOU GET 12 MILLION VOTES, AND YOU THERE — YOU GET TWO....

BALLOT

IMAGINE! STREAMLINED ELECTIONS IN WHICH WE JUST VOTE OUR BANK BALANCES! A.T.M.'s WILL REPLACE THOSE OLD POLLING BOOTHS — VERY THIRD WAVE!

CITIBANK

Vote Here

ATM

IN EARLY RETURNS JAMES DOE IS AHEAD BUT THE COUNT FROM CALIFORNIA, ARIZONA, EXXON AND MICROSOFT HAS YET TO COME IN....

IT'S TIME TO PUT THE WISDOM OF THE FREEMARKET IN THE BALLOT BOX! IN AMERICA YOU'RE ENTITLED TO ALL THE FREE SPEECH YOU CAN AFFORD... WHY NOT ALL THE VOTES YOU CAN AFFORD PEOPLE WHO DON'T HAVE MONEY DON'T DESERVE TO VOTE — PEOPLE WITH LOTS OF MONEY DESERVE LOTS OF VOTES.

MONEY'S ALWAYS TALKED. IT'S TIME IT GOT THE VOTE !!!

24

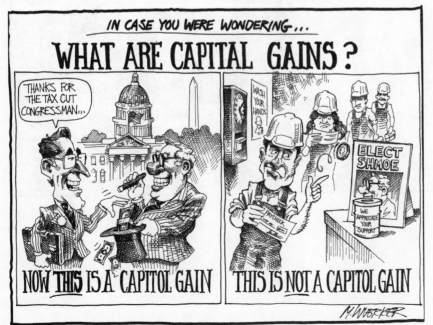

27

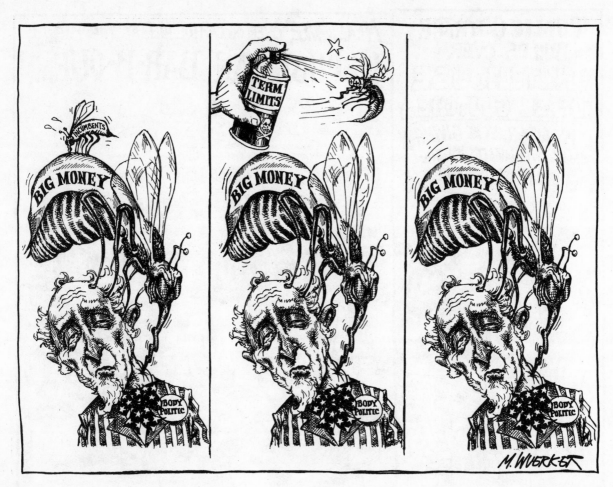

CHAPTER 3

PAX AMERICANA INC.

AFTA' NAFTA....

35

38

CHAPTER 4

SCAPEGOATS AND PITCHFORKS

Arise All Ye Bigots and Boneheads

A MODEST PROPOSAL

PERHAPS THE TIME HAS COME TO CHANGE THE SYMBOL OF THE G.O.P. FROM THE ELEPHANT TO...

G.O.P.

BLAME THOSE COUNTERCULTURE FEMINAZI CRAZED ENVIRONMENTALIST-WACKO UNWED TEENAGE MILITANT HOMOSEXUAL McGOVERNIKS!...

THE SCAPEGOATER

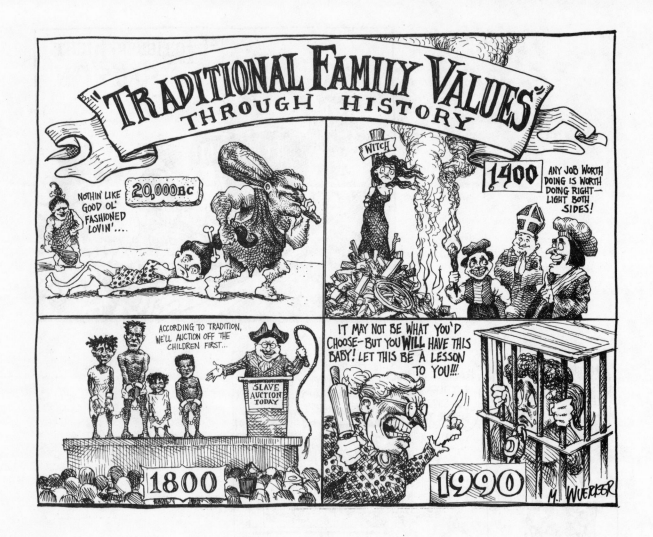

46

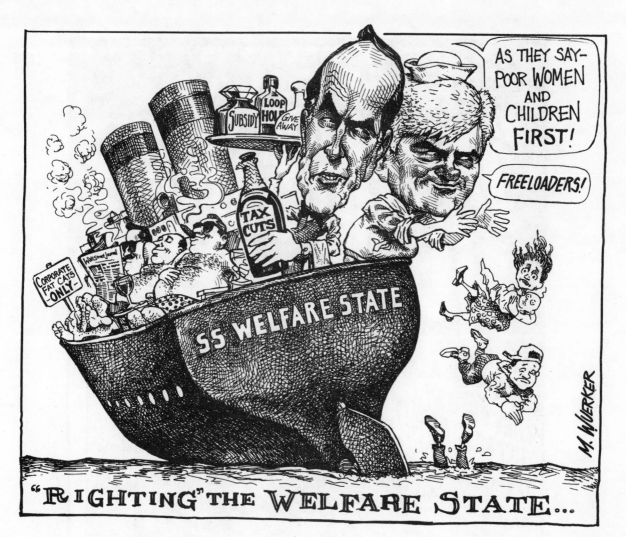

THE FATHER

THE SONS

THE HOLEY GHOSTS

I AM THE NRA

I AM GOD

Colt

SAVE THE UNBORN

M WUERKER

AMERICA DOESN'T NEED THE N.E.A. WHAT AMERICA **NEEDS** IS AN AYATOLLAH OF THE ARTS

NOW Y'ALL LISTEN CLOSE... THIS HERE IS ART! ANY QUESTIONS?

HELMS

ELVIS

M WUERKER

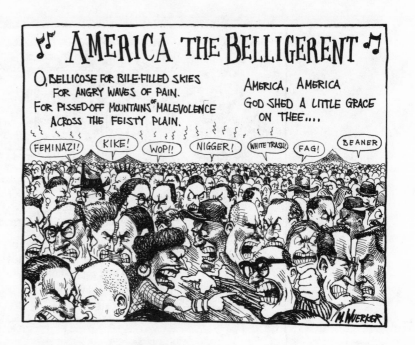

62

CHAPTER 5

THE TRIUMPH OF THE "FREE" MARKET

> THE FREE MARKET WORKS IN MYSTERIOUS WAYS....

"THE LEVEL PLAYING FIELD"

AFFIRMATIVE ACTION

M. WUERKER

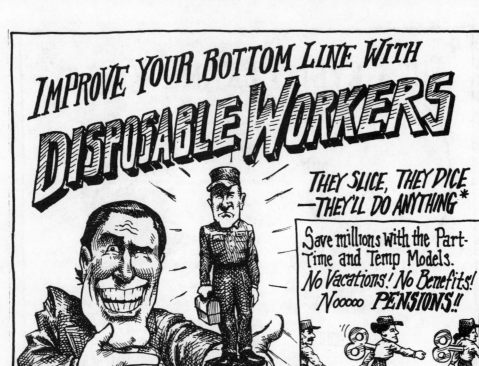

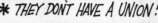

68

* Mattel Toys cut 3,174 jobs in 1997 while its C.E.O. raked in $10.7 million in compensation——News Item

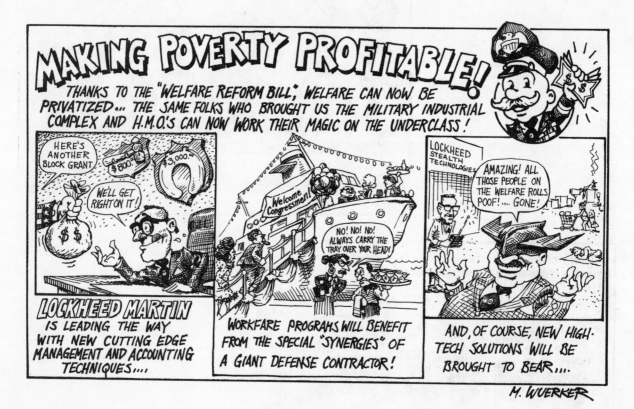

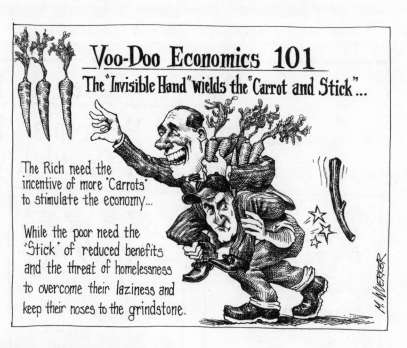

THE FREE ENTERPRISE SYSTEM SAILS ON...

GLOBOCORP

IN 1960 THE AVERAGE C.E.O. WAS PAID 41 TIMES MORE THAN THE AVERAGE WORKER. BY 1997 THE AVERAGE C.E.O. WAS PAID <u>326</u> TIMES MORE.[1]

1.) Business Week's 1997 Executive Pay Survey. April 20, 1998.

78

CHAPTER 6

♪ WE ARM THE WORLD ♪

M. WUERKER

84

CHAPTER 7

IT'S THE ENVIRONMENT *STUPID*.

THE BRIGHTER SIDE OF...

ENVIRONMENTAL DESTRUCTION

Realizing that, if enough of the Polar Ice Cap were to melt, Nevada could become prime beachfront real estate...

BLACK FLAG

SPRAY GLUE

SPRAY PAINT

AQUA NET

The McDoogans of Winnemucca resolve to do their part...and go to work on the Ozone Layer.

M. WUERKER

93

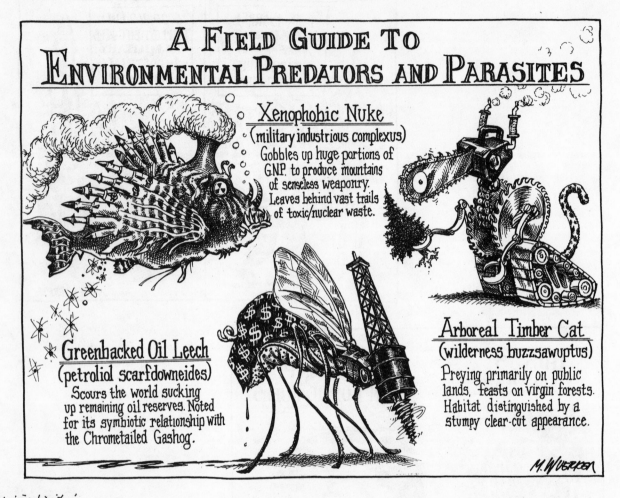

104

These are "throw-away" newspapers, burger wrappers, junk-mail, magazines, that are made from.....

....these "throw-away" trees, that grow in....

.... these "throw-away" rainforests, that are part of...

.....this "throw-away" Planet.

M. WUERKER

CHAPTER 8

MEDIA INDUSTRIAL COMPLEX

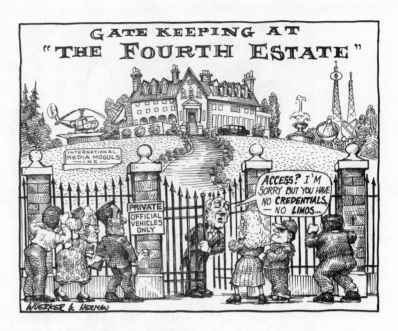

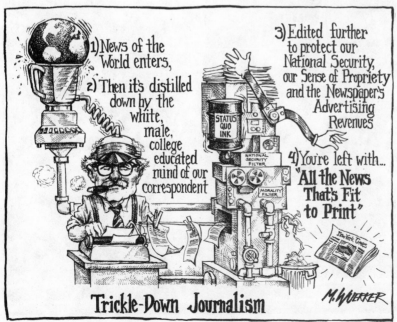

110

If a tree fell in the woods, and nobody from the New York Times was there to cover it, would it make a sound?

fig a.

THE FOREST, Sept. 2—
A Tree fell down and went boom today.

fig b.

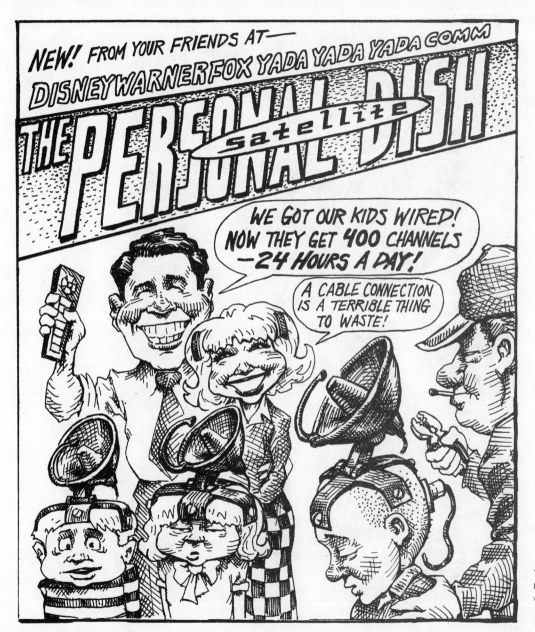

CONTINUE FLIP BOOK ☞ HERE